Making Faces

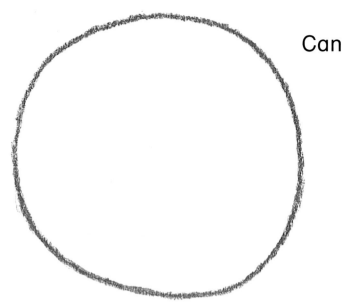

Can you draw a circle?

Now make it smile.

Paint it yellow like the sun.

Try making circle faces on your paper.
Add ears and hair and funny hats.

This is a happy frog.

This is a sad frog.

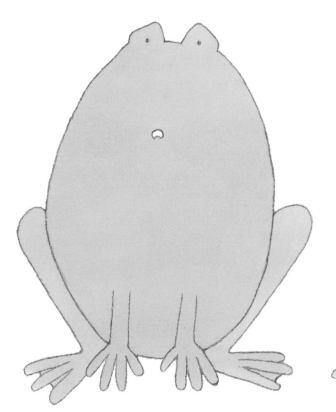

This frog is puzzled.

This frog is laughing.

Now can you draw your own faces?

9

Here is a sad monkey.

Here is a happy monkey.

This monkey is laughing.

This monkey is shouting.

Draw your own monkey faces.

Sally is . . .

sleeping

crying

eating

angry

Can you draw your own people with different faces?

Number
and
Word Pictures

If you can
do a two . . .

you can draw
a swan!

14

What can *you* make with a figure 3? 15

If you can make a six . . .

you can draw a pelican. Now you try.

18

19

Make a nine into a can.

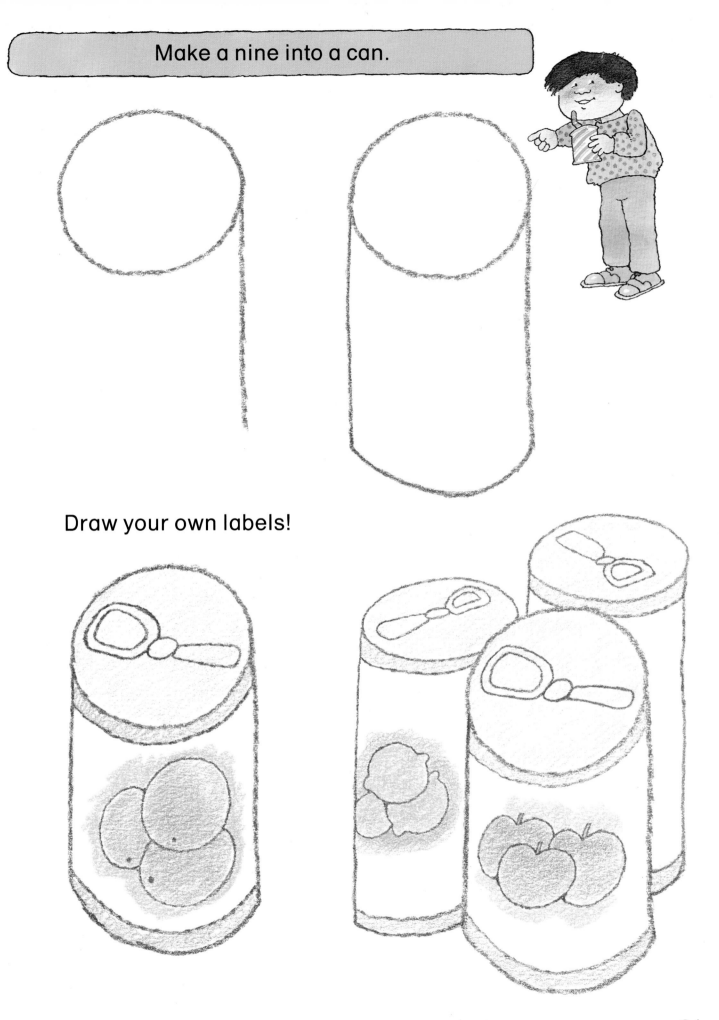

Draw your own labels!

Time for you to try.

Leon Baxter

Can you write your name in pictures?

Helpful
Squares

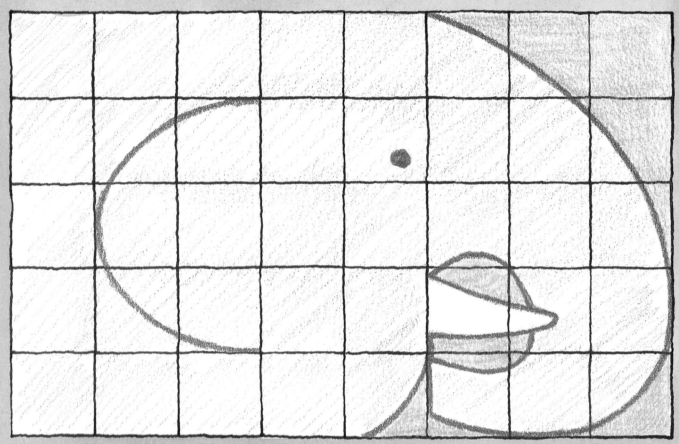

Here is a picture of an elephant.
Can you make an elephant of your own?

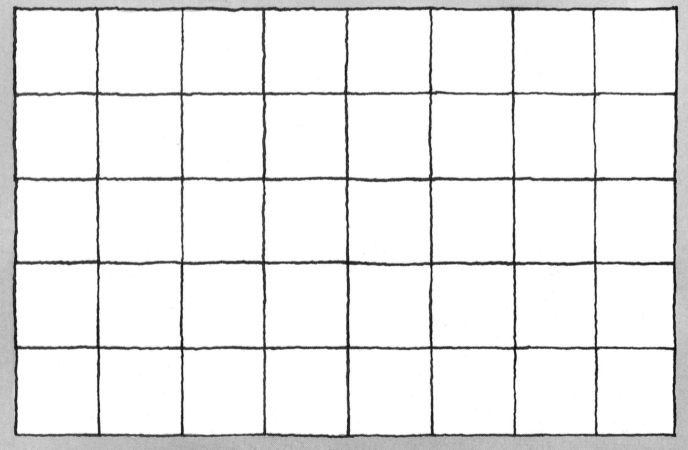

TRACE these squares and use them to help you.

1 Here is a picture of a car.

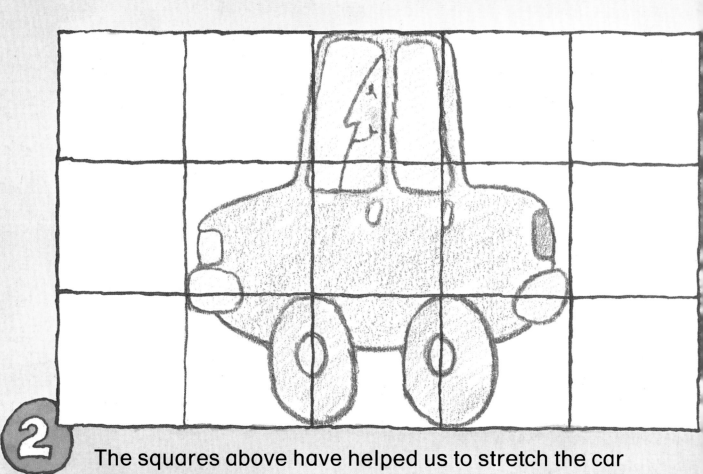

2 The squares above have helped us to stretch the car up and down.

3 Here the squares have helped us to stretch it from side to side.

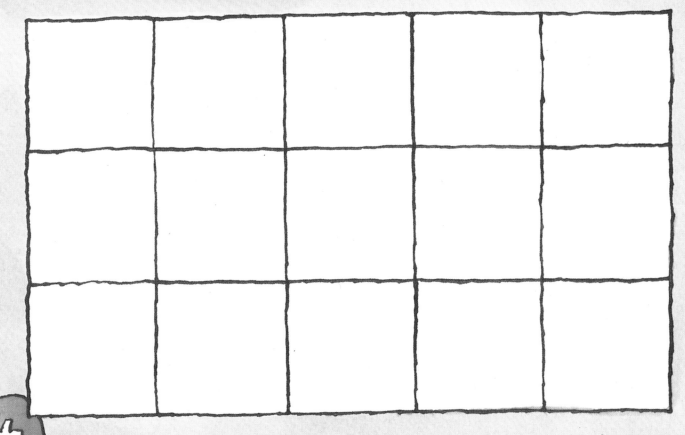

4 Now can you TRACE these squares and use them to draw the car the way *you* like it?

1 Here is a picture of an elephant.

2 Now I have made it longer.

28

3 Here I have made it shorter.

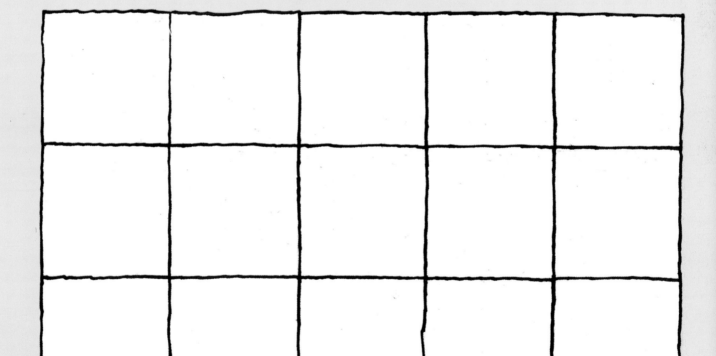

4 TRACE these squares to draw an elephant that *you* like.

Shapes
in
Nature

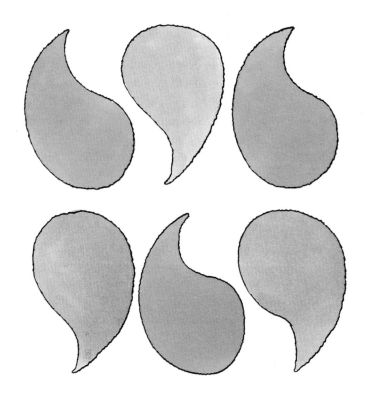

Rainfall

Rainfall is part of a well-designed plan in nature. The sun shining over the sea makes water rise and form clouds. The clouds then move over the land where the water falls from the clouds as rain. Clouds come in all shapes and sizes.

Clouds and rain are fun to draw.

Look at all these cloud shapes.

Now draw your own.

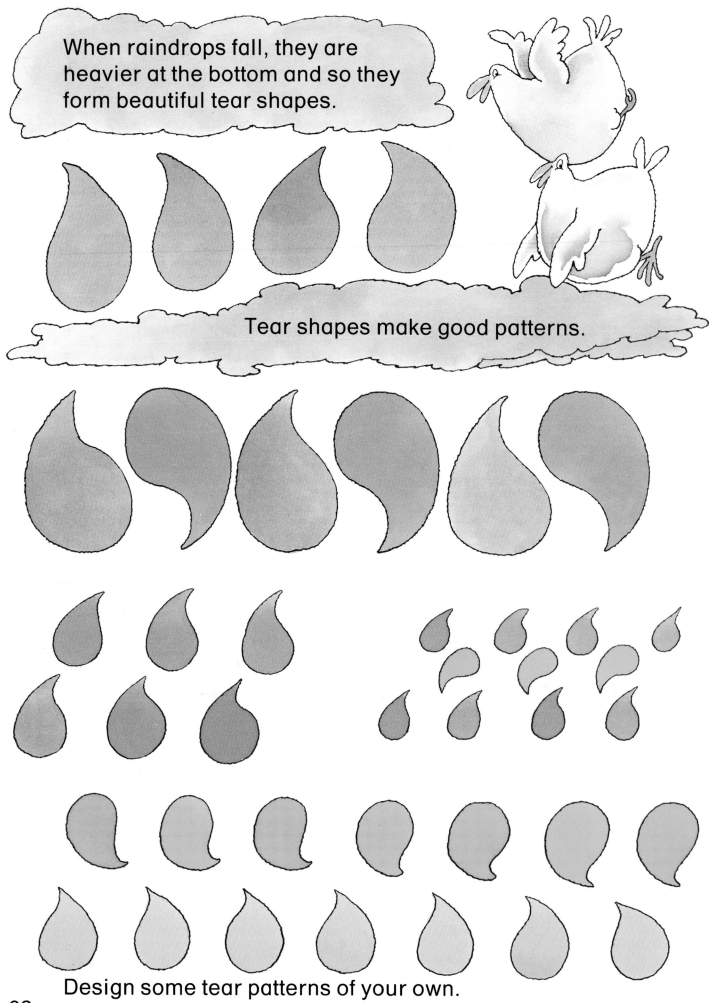

When raindrops fall, they are heavier at the bottom and so they form beautiful tear shapes.

Tear shapes make good patterns.

Design some tear patterns of your own.

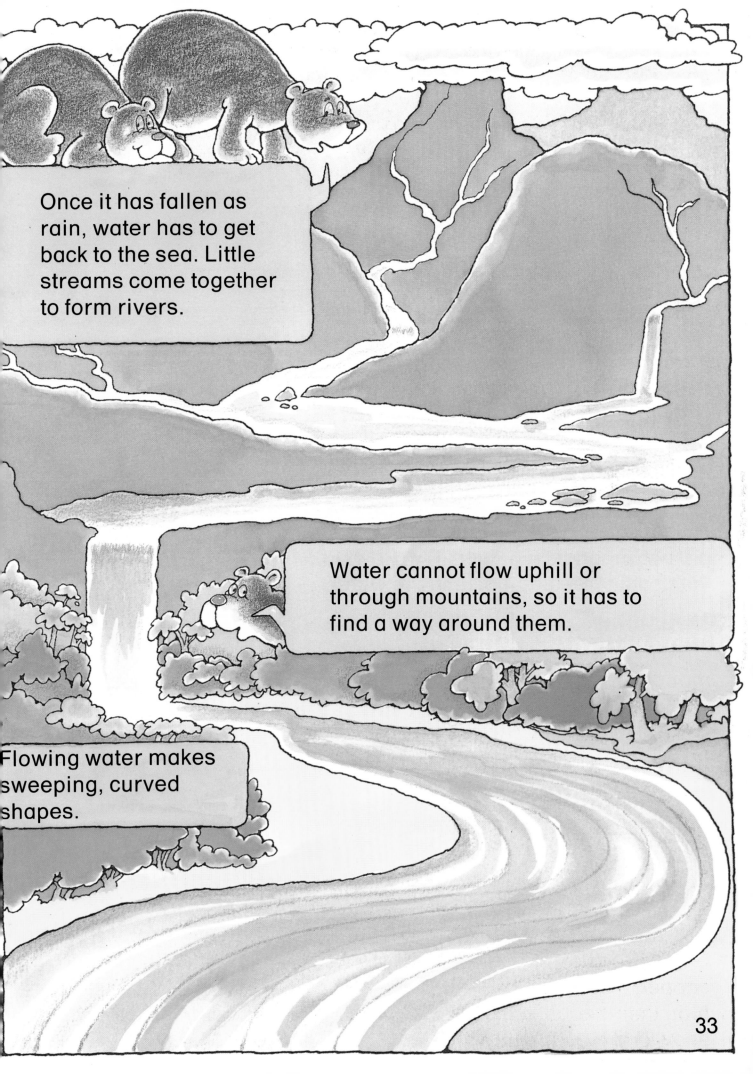

Once it has fallen as rain, water has to get back to the sea. Little streams come together to form rivers.

Water cannot flow uphill or through mountains, so it has to find a way around them.

Flowing water makes sweeping, curved shapes.

33

Rivers

Rivers can be fast and noisy or slow and lazy. This is a slow, meandering river. Try drawing a river with some trees reflected in the water.

Mountains

I live in the mountains.

Some are snow-capped and some hide their heads in the clouds. Can you draw a mountain range with snow and clouds?

Mountains rise high into the sky.

Draw them as separate huge shapes. The peaks behind are far away.

Flowers and plants

In order to live, flowers must grow roots downwards to drink, and leaves and petals upwards and outwards to reach the sun. All flowers obey these rules, but they come in lots of different shapes, colours and sizes.

rose

tulip

I have drawn two flowers.

A tree must grow roots firmly down into the ground and branches out and up, so that the sun can shine on its leaves. These too grow in different shapes and sizes – some are broad and flat and some are thin and pointed.

oak

yew

I have drawn two leaves.

Can you draw your favourite flowers and leaves?

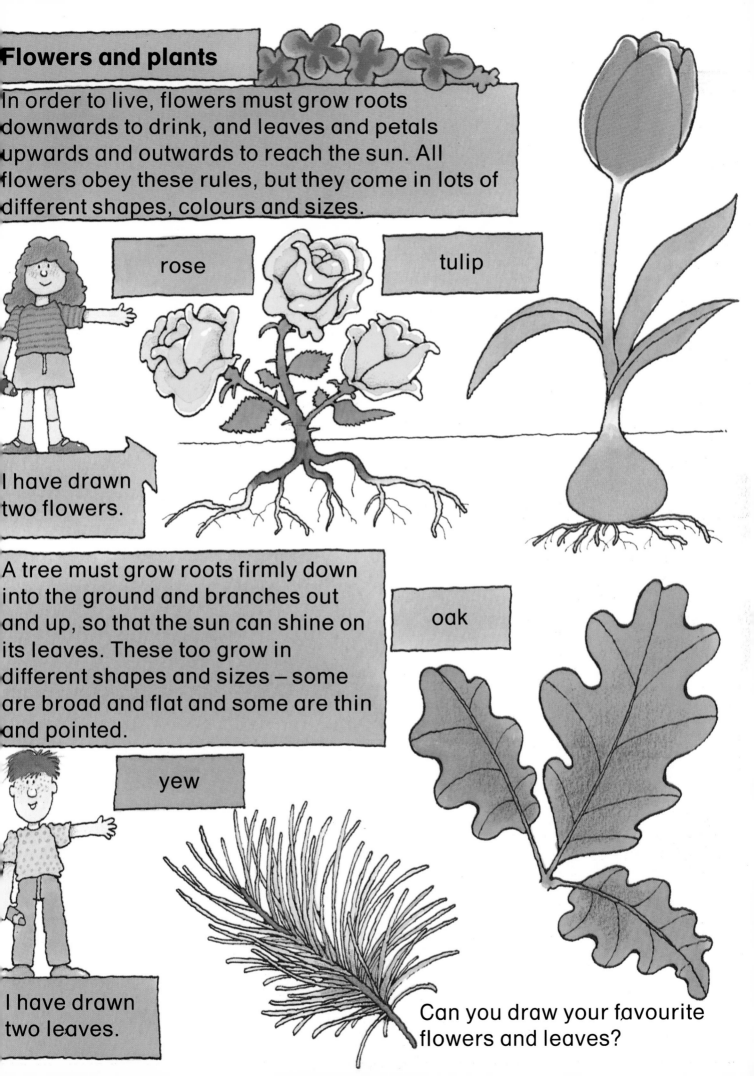

Often plants are small shapes that form together to make larger symmetrical shapes.

Sometimes little flowers grow closely together to form multi-flower heads.

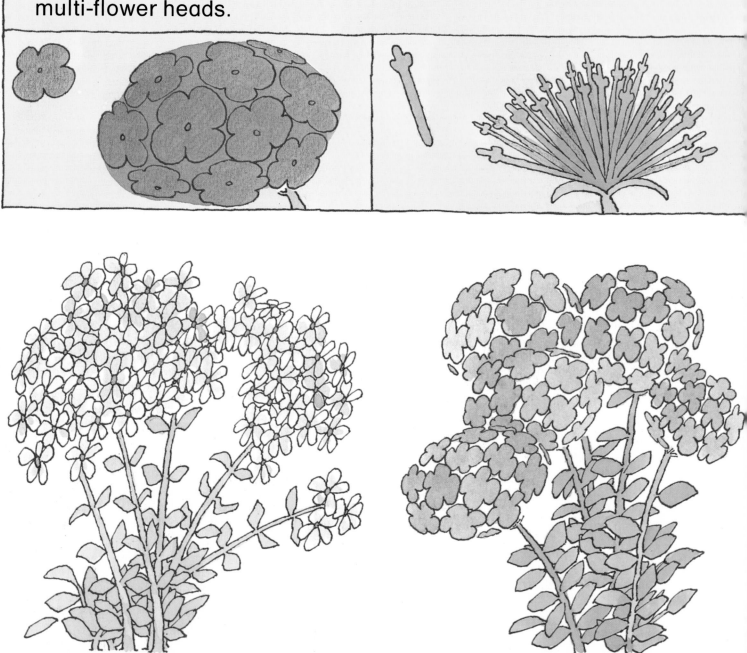

Can you draw groups of plants together? Think of the ways they might lean and bend.

Horizons
and
Perspective

Skyline pictures

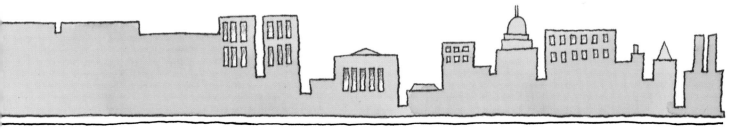

Without taking your pencil or brush from the paper, draw a line like this:

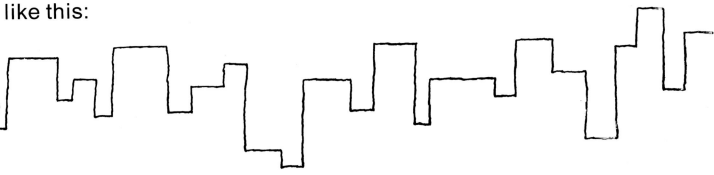

Add towers, roofs, domes and windows.

Try it again using more than one line.

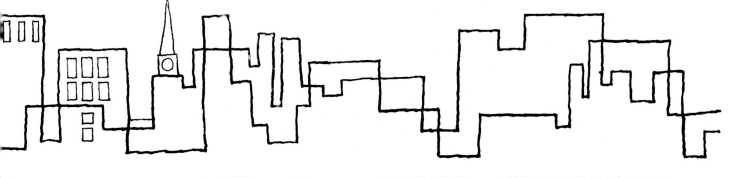

Can you draw some skylines of your own?

Drawing a view

To draw a view you need guidelines on which to build your picture.

1. This artist is drawing his eye-level.

2. This artist has a high eye-level.

3. This artist has a low eye-level.

Parallel lines are lines that stay the same distance apart like this:

The sides of a road are usually parallel lines. In these pictures the sides of the road are parallel, but they look as if they meet. They appear to meet at a point on the eye level. This is called the *vanishing* point.

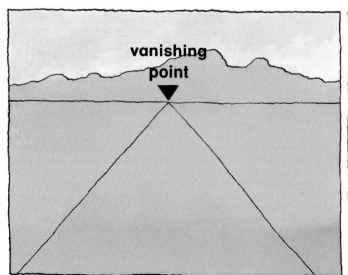 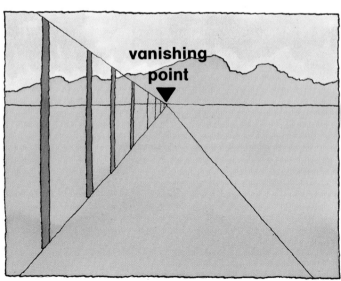

Distant colours

When you look into the distance,
colours seem to fade.

Which areas look close to you and which areas look far away?

A red car sets off down the road. The colour of the car appears to fade as it moves away.

Now you choose two colours. Can you create close areas and distant areas?

The city

Choose your own eye level and vanishing point and draw a city. If you take your eye level down, the buildings will look taller.

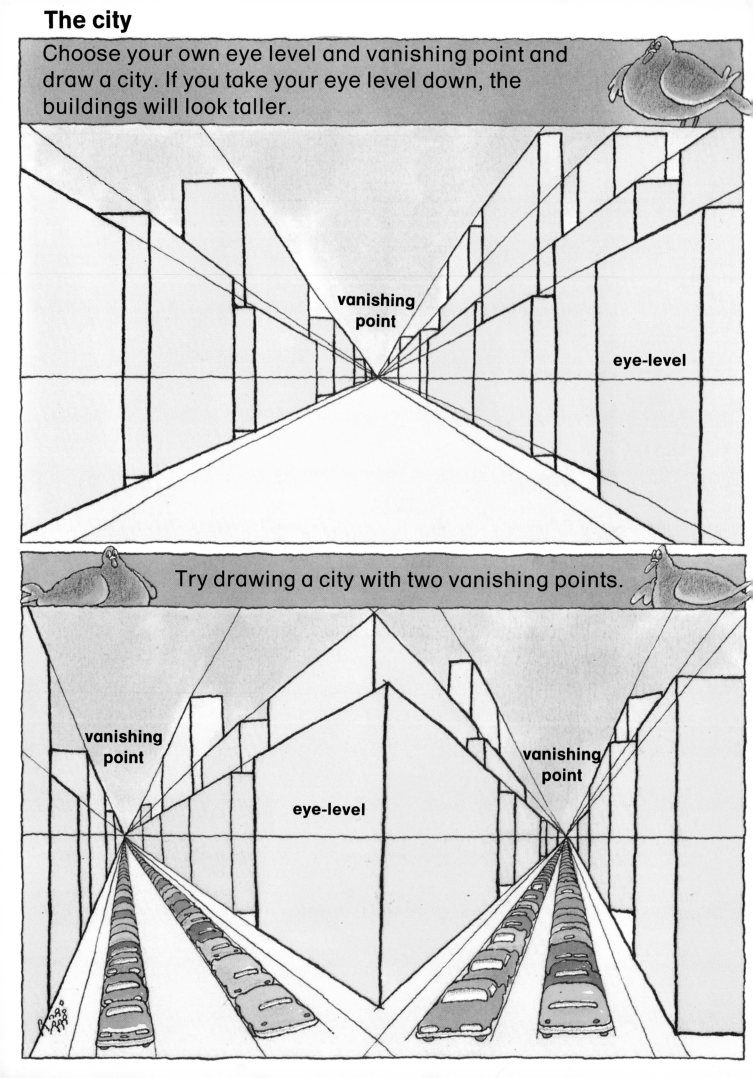

vanishing point

eye-level

Try drawing a city with two vanishing points.

vanishing point

eye-level

vanishing point

Drawing People

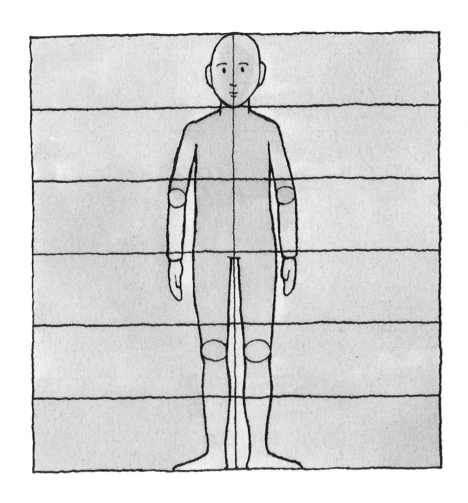

This section is about drawing people. To do this, we have to know about the proportions and measurements of the body.

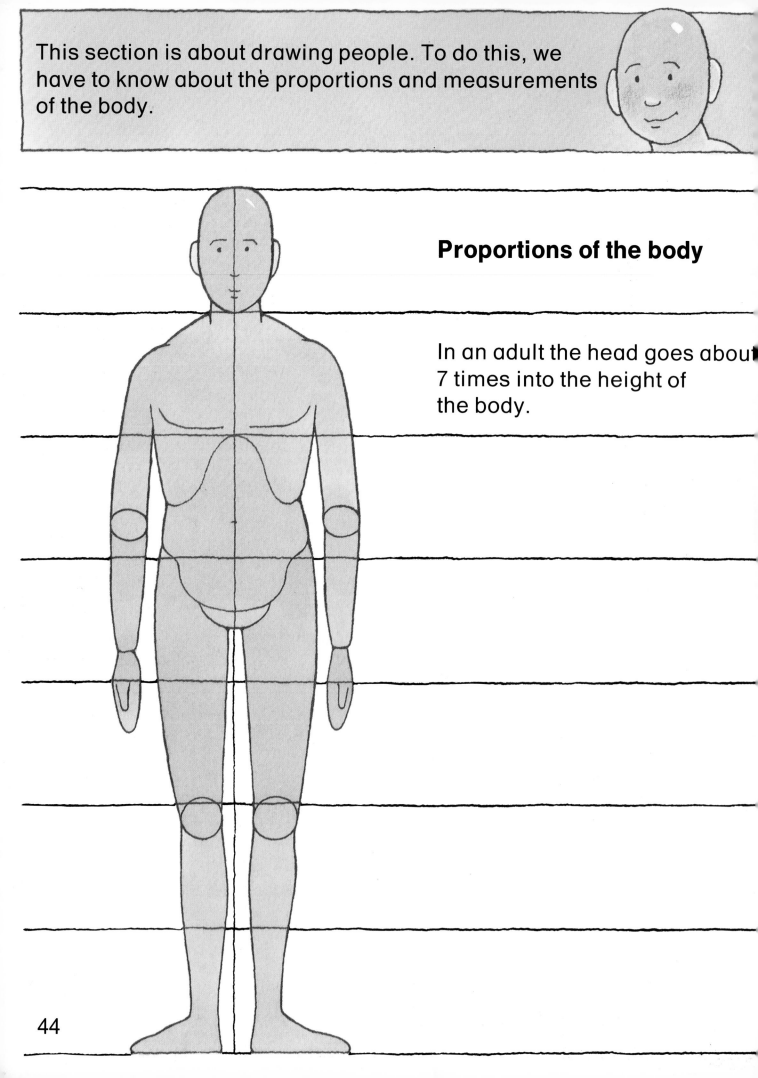

Proportions of the body

In an adult the head goes about 7 times into the height of the body.

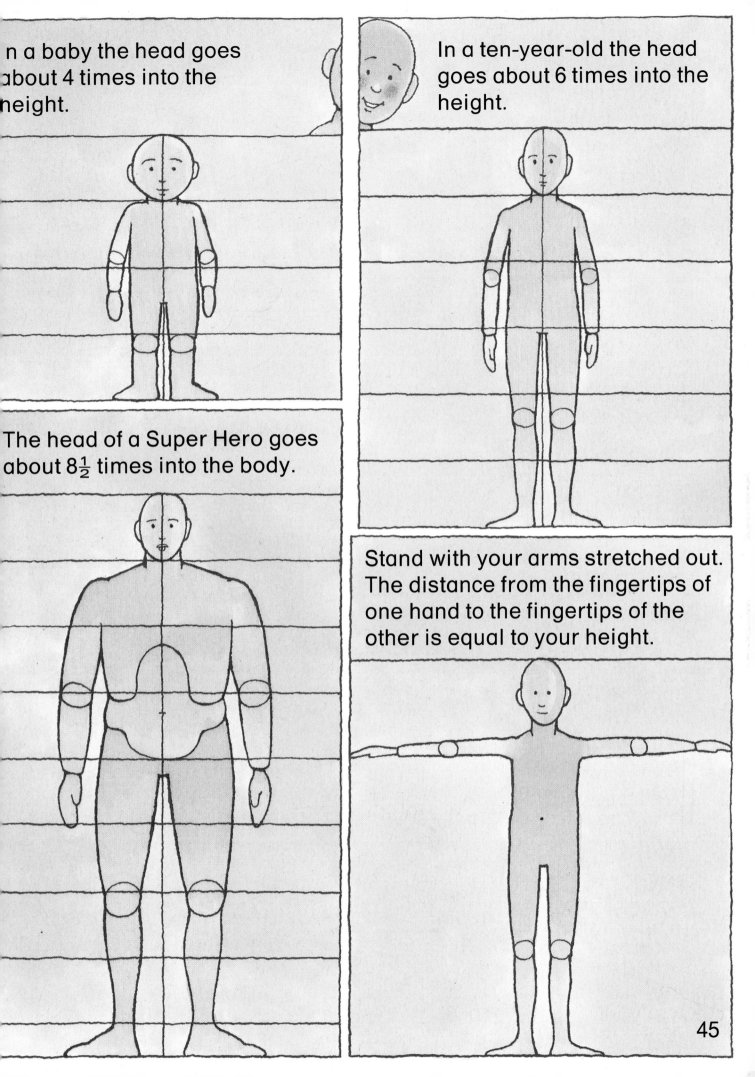

In a baby the head goes about 4 times into the height.

In a ten-year-old the head goes about 6 times into the height.

The head of a Super Hero goes about $8\frac{1}{2}$ times into the body.

Stand with your arms stretched out. The distance from the fingertips of one hand to the fingertips of the other is equal to your height.

Proportions *do* vary, so find a model and do some measuring for yourself.

Hold your pencil or brush like this:

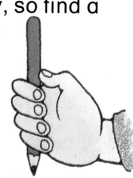

The tip of your thumb will be able to slide up and down.

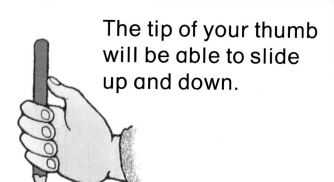

Keep your arm straight, hold up your pencil or brush and by moving your thumb up and down you can find the height of your model's head.

Hold up your pencil or brush so that the top is in line with the top of the model's head.

Now slide your thumb so that the tip of your thumb is in line with the chin.

head height

Keep your thumb still and your pencil or brush upright; use the head as a unit of measurement and find out how many times the head will go into your model's head.

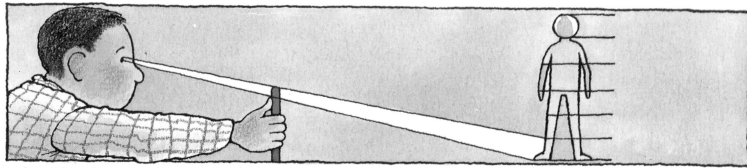

Look at your family and friends and make pictures of them.

Proportions of the head

Ears are in line with eyebrows at the top, and tip of the nose at the bottom.

The hairline is about one-third down from the top of the head to the eyes.

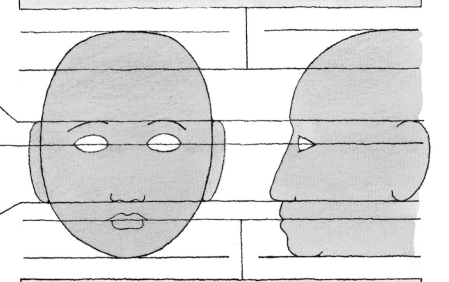

Eyes are halfway down the head.

The tip of the nose is halfway between the eyes and the chin.

The mouth is about one-third of the way between the nose and the chin.

Follow these guidelines when you want to draw a head which is turned away from you.

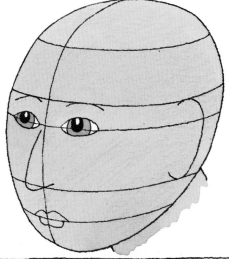

By laying your pencil on a drawing, you can use your forefinger and thumb to measure and check distances.

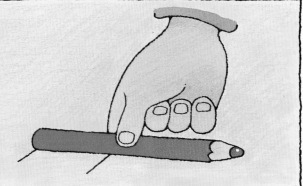

Hands and feet

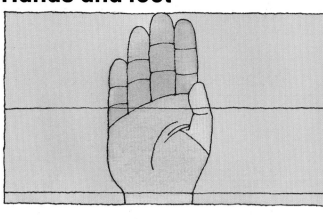

Look at your hand and see where the tip of each finger is in relation to the others. Notice the shape and position of the thumb.

Can you draw these hands?

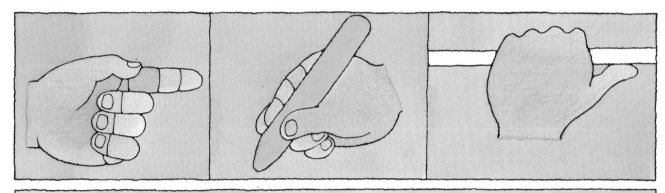

Look at the shape of a foot. See how it flattens out towards the end.

These are construction lines.

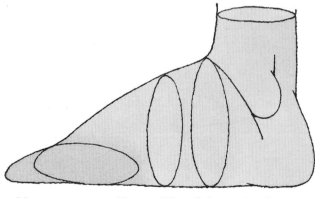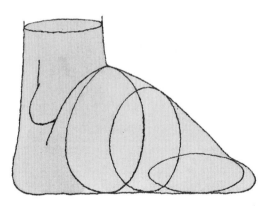

You can use lines like this to help you learn about the shape of a foot.

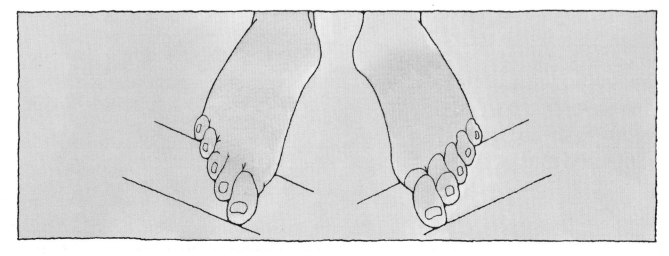

Foreshortening

If you draw someone by using cylinders you can work out the parts of the body quite easily.

Turn a cylinder towards you and it appears to grow shorter. This is called foreshortening.

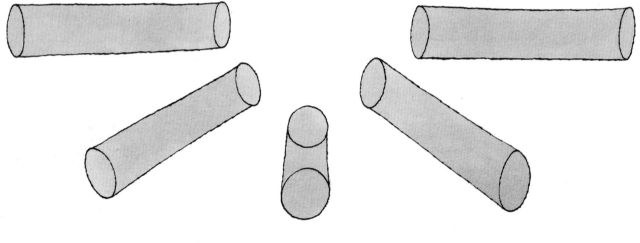

This girl's arms are really the same length. Her left arm is coming towards you but because of its position it looks as if it is shorter.

Weight watching

There is so much information to put down when you draw a person. How do you begin?

The boy in picture A is our model. Let's ignore details like face and clothes and make a basic drawing showing *how* he is sitting.

The arrows show where his weight is being supported.

A

I have imagined I can see his spine and drawn the basic frame on which I can build my picture.

Add the other arm and the legs.

Now I can put flesh on him with cylinders.

Try drawing some cylinder people.

Making a portrait gallery

Sometimes it's not good to plan pictures. Try fun portraits of your family and friends. These are two of my favourite relatives.

Aunt Battren

Uncle Baldwin

Drawing Animals

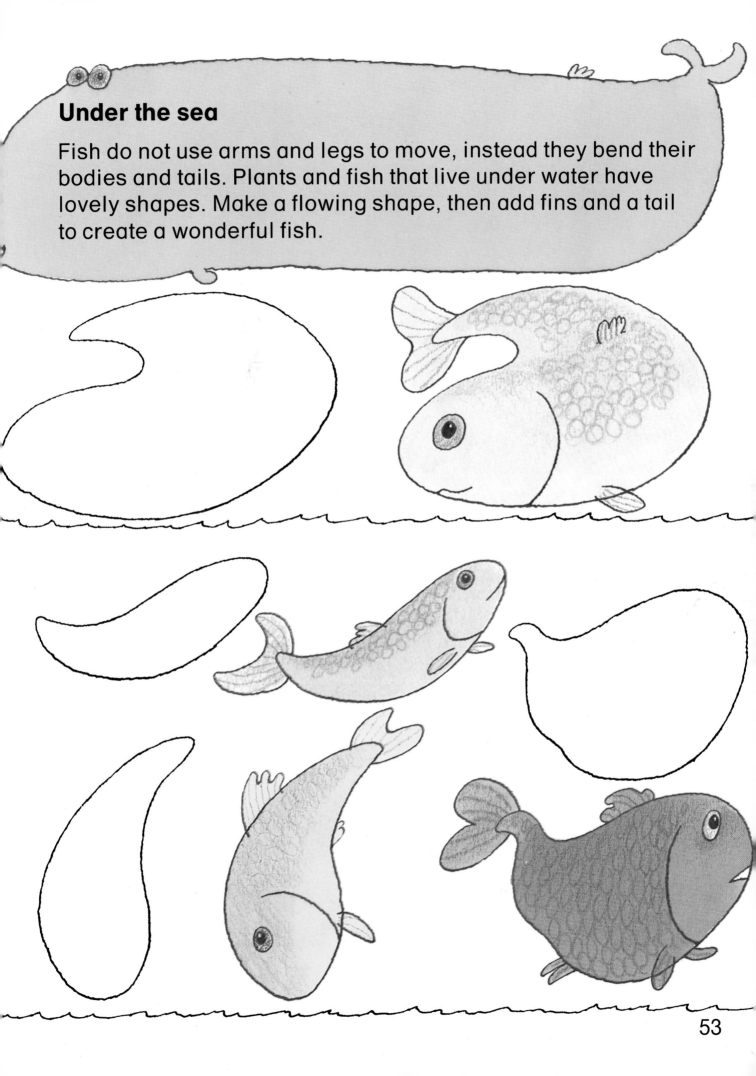

Under the sea

Fish do not use arms and legs to move, instead they bend their bodies and tails. Plants and fish that live under water have lovely shapes. Make a flowing shape, then add fins and a tail to create a wonderful fish.

Dog

I have used simple shapes to draw this dog and its puppies.

Cat

Look at the shapes I have used to draw a cat and kittens.

Try drawing some of your own dogs and cats.

Drawing a basic bird

Birds have skeletons similar to ours. This girl is standing as if she were a bird.

Birds have two fingers and a thumb within the structure of their wings.

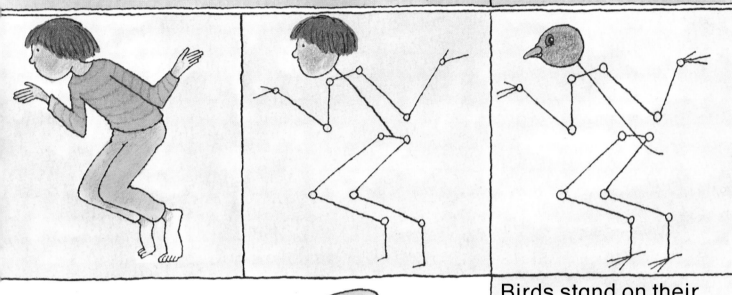

Birds stand on their toes. Most birds have three forward toes and one back toe.

They have deep chests for the powerful muscles that move their wings.

Try drawing birds of different sizes.

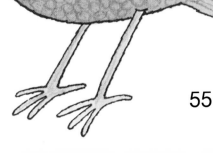

Horses   Many animals stand on their toes. They have the same joints as we do but in different places.

The top half of a horse's limbs are part of its body.

This boy is standing as if he were a horse.

The knee is our wrist.
↳

elbow

knee

heel

knee

The hock is our heel

If a horse stood like you it would look like this:

See if you can draw a horse.

Action

Action!

Here is a picture sequence.
It tells an action story.

The action is shown by bending and stretching lines and by drawing something about to happen or that has happened.
This gives the suggestion of time.

How to suggest time

In these three pictures we can show:

before

1. He is going to kick the ball.

during

2. He is kicking the ball.

after

3. He has kicked the ball.

before

1. She is going to throw the ball.

during

2. She is throwing the ball.

after

3. She has thrown the ball.

Can you make up your own sequence pictures?

Action sequences

Look at these two picture sequences. One series of actions takes place in a short space of time, while the other is over a much longer period.

By changing backgrounds, and showing means of travel, you can suggest time passing. Now draw your own holiday sequence.

Movie – making

These men are filming a stuntman
driving a car over a cliff.

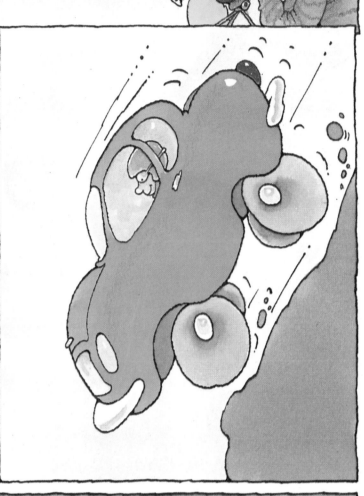

Create your own favourite action
scene in four frames.

INDEX